TENOR

CONTEMPORARY THEATRE SONGS

D1082228

SONGS FROM THE 21ST CENTURY

ISBN 978-1-4950-7154-6

7777 W. BLUEMOUND RD. P.O. BOX 13819 MILWAUKEE, WI 53213

Visit Hal Leonard Online at
www.halleonard.com

ABOUT THE SONGS AND SHOWS

ALADDIN (Broadway 2014)
Music by Alan Menken
Lyrics by Howard Ashman, Tim Rice, and Chad Beguelin

Aladdin is based on the 1992 Disney animated feature of the same name. In the fictional Middle Eastern city of Agrabah, Aladdin is orphaned and homeless, and survives by stealing food from street vendors. However, he vows to mend his ways at the beginning of the musical to stop being a "worthless street rat" and to make his deceased mother **"Proud of Your Boy."** This is one of three songs with lyrics by Howard Ashman not used in the film but incorporated into the stage musical score.

AMAZING GRACE (Broadway 2015)
Music and Lyrics by Christopher Smith

The musical *Amazing Grace* tells of the dramatic life of John Newton (1725–1807), the man who wrote the words to the popular hymn of the show's title. Just before Christmas 1742, Newtown's slave-trader father arrives. He is angry that his son has rejected the life prescribed for him (**"Truly Alive"**). Forced into the British Navy, Newton falls into the ocean during battle, and he is captured and imprisoned in Sierra Leone. John is able to stay alive by advising his captor Princess Peyai on how to better run her slave-trading empire. He eventually gives up this life and fights for abolitionism.

BIG FISH (Broadway 2013)
Music and Lyrics by Andrew Lippa

The big-hearted musical *Big Fish* is based on the original 1998 novel by Daniel Wallace, as well as the 2003 film adaptation by John August (who also wrote the book for the musical). The main characters are Edward Bloom, his wife Sandra and their son William. Edward has spent his life regaling Will with fanciful tales of his past, including a story about a giant fish that jumped into a man's arms after Edward taught the fisherman to catch fish by doing the "Alabama Stomp." Scenes jump between the present and the past, interspersed with Edward's fanciful tales. Will and his new wife, Josephine, live in New York City and have recently dicovered they are expecting a child. When Will finds out that his future child will be a boy, he vows to improve his relationship with his father as he sings **"Stranger."** Because of Edward's constant storytelling, Will feels that he doesn't truly know his father. Edward eventually dies of cancer, and by his funeral, Will has learned that all of his father's tales were in fact based in truth.

THE BRIDGES OF MADISON COUNTY (Broadway 2014)
Music and Lyrics by Jason Robert Brown

The Bridges of Madison County tells the story of an Italian immigrant "war bride," Francesca, on a farm near Winterset, Iowa, in 1965. While her husband and children are away at a 4-H fair, a *National Geographic* photographer, on assignment to shoot the historical covered bridges of the county, knocks on her door asking for directions. The photographer, Robert, and Francesca have an almost immediate connection that results in a brief but intense affair. Francesca and Robert fall deeply in love. Many years pass. Francesca's husband dies. Francesca was never again in contact with Robert, who waited for her call his entire life. He has retired from working due to an illness. He arranges for a letter to Francesca to be sent to her after his death with a picture he took of her on the bridge. He sings **"It All Fades Away"** as an older man near the end of his life. The musical is based on the 1993 novel of the same name by Robert James Waller. A film version was released in 1995, starring Meryl Streep and Clint Eastwood.

BRIGHT STAR (Broadway 2016)
Music by Stephen Martin and Edie Brickell
Lyrics by Edie Brickell

Bright Star is set in the Blue Ridge Mountains of North Carolina. The action alternates between the years 1945 and 1923. In 1923, sixteen-year-old Alice Murphy begins a romance with a young man named Jimmy Ray Dobbs. They make love and Alice becomes pregnant. Jimmy's father, Josiah, the mayor of their town, secretly pretends to put the baby up for adoption. Alice learns this soon after giving birth. Despite her protests, Josiah departs on a train with the baby. He places the baby in a suitcase and throws it into a river when no one is looking. Much later, Josiah confesses to his son what happened. Jimmy Ray can't bear to tell Alice the news (**"Heartbreaker"**).

BRING IT ON: THE MUSICAL (Broadway 2012)
Music by Lin-Manuel Miranda and Tom Kitt
Lyrics by Amanda Green and Lin-Manuel Miranda

Bring It On: The Musical was inspired by the 2000 film *Bring It On*, about competitive cheerleading and high school rivalries. The story focuses on Campbell Davis, a former cheerleading captain who has been transferred to a new school that has no cheerleading. Campbell leads the dance squad, the Queen Bees, to compete against her old classmates at a regional cheerleading competition. Randall, the school D.J., develops a crush on Campbell and asks her out on a date. She is distraught and angry at herself for lying to the Queen Bees about the prize for the competition being college tuition. Randall cheers her up with **"Enjoy the Trip,"** about how to enjoy and make the most of life. Originally a duet with Campbell, the song has been edited as a solo for this volume.

DIRTY ROTTEN SCOUNDRELS (Broadway 2005; London 2014)
Music and Lyrics by David Yazbek

Dirty Rotten Scoundrels is based on the 1988 film starring Michael Caine and Steve Martin, which itself was a remake of the 1964 film *Bedtime Story*. Two independent con men prey upon lonely, wealthy women vacationing on the French Riviera. The suave, British Lawrence Jameson poses as a rich, deposed prince who needs funds to fight revolutionaries. Crass American Freddy Benson tries to usurp the female fortune through a sob story. The two grifters decide that the small town on the French Riviera isn't big enough for both of them. They choose a mark, Christine Colgate, the "American Soap Queen." Whoever gets to her money first will get to remain in town. In the end, after many double-crosses, Christine swindles them both. **"Great Big Stuff"** is the entertaining and shifty Freddy's boastful first song in Act I. After he spots Lawrence as a con man and confronts him at his expensive home, Freddy wants Lawrence to teach him everything so that he can live in luxury and get great big stuff too.

THE DROWSY CHAPERONE (Broadway 2006; London 2007)
Music and Lyrics by Lisa Lambert, Greg Morrison

This show-within-a-show features a rather sour character simply called the Man in Chair, who escapes his depression by obsessively playing an old recording of a 1928 musical, *The Drowsy Chaperone*. Its story is of an actress, Janet Van De Graaff (Sutton Foster in the original cast), indulgent in vanity, engaged to a man she has only recently met. The show, characters, story and songs are an affectionate send-up of stage and screen clichés. Through it all the Man in Chair gets swept up in the action, and comments to the audience. At one point a Latin lothario, Aldolpho, has been enlisted to seduce Janet and stop the wedding. He enters her room, which currently occupied by Janet's middle-aged, heavy-drinking Chaperone. Thinking she is Janet, he introduces himself in **"I Am Aldolpho."**

EVER AFTER *(2015)*
Music by Zina Goldrich
Lyrics by Marcy Heisler

Ever After received its world premiere in 2015 at the Paper Mill Playhouse, a major regional theater in Milburn, New Jersey, just across the river from Manhattan. The musical, based on the 1998 film starring Drew Barrymore, is a retelling of the classic Cinderella story, this time with a more empowered heroine. As in the traditional story, Danielle (the Cinderella character) is left with her cruel stepmother and stepsister following her father's death. In **"Right Before My Eyes"** Danielle struggles with the truth as Prince Henry declares she is the love of his life, and vows to tell the world at the masque.

THE FULL MONTY *(Broadway 2000; London 2002, 2009)*
Music and Lyrics by David Yazbek

Based on the successful British movie of the same name, *The Full Monty* was David Yazbek's first foray into Broadway. The scene for the stage musical is changed to Buffalo, New York. The men in the story are unemployed workers. Determined to support themselves and their families, the decidedly average group form a Chippendale's type strip act, baring everything (as the British phrase "the full monty" implies) for entertainment and cash. Each of the guys has a personal obstacle to overcome, and the act of stripping publicly becomes a symbol of freedom and pride, rather than the embarrassment it once seemed. Early in the show Jerry sings **"Man"** to his buddy Dave in response to his emasculated feelings, seeing the relative power and success of his ex-wife and other wives of unemployed men.

A GENTLEMAN'S GUIDE TO LOVE AND MURDER *(Broadway 2013)*
Music by Steven Lutvak
Lyrics by Robert L. Freedman and Steven Lutvak

The musical comedy *A Gentleman's Guide to Love and Murder* is based on the 1907 novel *Israel Rank: The Autobiography of a Criminal* by Roy Horniman. The style of the light-hearted musical recalls operetta and the British music hall. The main character is Monty Navarro, a young man in London who grew up in poverty, but is informed following the death of his mother that she was a member of the noble D'Ysquith family, and that he is ninth in line to be the Earl of Highhurst. He schemes to murder those relatives who stand in his way in a series of what appear to be freak accidents. Monty is in love with Sibella. She is also in love with Monty, but she will not marry him because he is poor. Instead she decides marries the likelier prospect Lionel Holland. Despite being married, Monty and Sibella carry on an affair. At the beginning of Act II Monty sings **"Sibella"** about his continued affection for her. He is soon arrested for the one murder he didn't commit. More plot twists occur before Monty's release from prison at the end of the show.

HAMILTON *(Off-Broadway 2015; Broadway 2015)*
Music and Lyrics by Lin-Manuel Miranda

Hamilton combines American history with hip-hop, and tells the story of Founding Father Alexander Hamilton's life from the onset of his career until his death. Early in the show, in 1776 the spirit of revolution is surging in the British American colonies. A loyal royalist preaches against the revolution, rebuked by the fervent Hamilton. A message arrives from King George III of England, reminding the colonists that he will send troops if he suspects the revolution is getting out hand, and suggesting that they will soon submit to the English monarch again. His song, **"You'll Be Back,"** shows his overconfidence, cluelessness and insouciant insensitivity. The story continues deep into American history of the Revolutionary War years and after, culminating in the death of Hamilton in a famous duel with his rival Aaron Burr.

HONEYMOON IN VEGAS (Broadway 2015)
Music and Lyrics by Jason Robert Brown

Honeymoon in Vegas is a musical comedy based on the 1992 movie of the same name. Jack and Betsy have been dating for five years. Betsy is ready to get married. Jack loves Betsy deeply but is troubled by the dying wish of his mother, which was that he would never marry because no woman could ever love him as much as she did. Jack finally decides he is ready, and the two travel to Las Vegas to get married. However, upon arrival the rich gambler Tommy Korman sees Betsy and decides he has to have her. He beats Jack in a fixed game of poker and when Jack can't pay up, he strikes a deal to be able to spend the weekend with Betsy. After being charmed by Tommy, Betsy flies off with him to his vacation home in Hawaii. A cross-pacific adventure ensues as Jack follows hot on their trail to get Betsy back. Jack sings **"Isn't That Enough?"** to his dead mother in Act II, and she finally grants him permission to marry Betsy if he is able to prove himself to "be a man." After some crazy plot twists Jack and Betsy marry in Las Vegas at the end of the show.

IF/THEN (Broadway 2014)
Music by Tom Kitt
Lyrics by Brian Yorkey

If/Then is a contemporary musical that features two parallel hypothetical paths that 40-year-old divorcée Elizabeth's life could take. Elizabeth has just moved to New York for a fresh start after a divorce. She meets up with her friends Kate, a lesbian kindergarten teacher, and Lucas, a bisexual community organizer, in Madison Square Park. Kate encourages Elizabeth to become a free spirit, seek out new experiences, and go by the name "Liz." Lucas says she should use "Beth" and focus on her career. The musical then splits off into two possible story lines, one following the life of Liz and the other of Beth. In Liz's story, an Army doctor named Josh approaches her first in a park, then on a subway. After a third meeting in the park, Josh admits he started spending more time there in the hope of running into her (**"You Never Know"**). After Beth and Lucas spend a night together, Beth doesn't want to start a relationship with him, but he tries to convince her in **"You Don't Need to Love Me."**

IT SHOULDA BEEN YOU (Broadway 2015)
Music by Barbara Anselmi
Lyrics by Brian Hargrove

It Shoulda Been You takes place at the wedding of Jewish Rebecca Steinberg and Christian Brian Howard. Near the beginning of the show, Rebecca's sister Jenny accidentally calls Rebecca's ex, Marty, who interprets this as a sign that he needs to stop the wedding. At one point, Jenny, sick of being mistreated by her stressed-out family, impulsively kisses Marty, who demands an explanation. He then confesses that he never loved Rebecca, but he did love Jenny. He offers the possibility of a romantic relationship with her if she wants it (**"Whatever"**).

THE LAST FIVE YEARS (Off-Broadway 2002)
Music and Lyrics by Jason Robert Brown

This two-person show chronicles the beginning, middle and deterioration of a relationship between a successful writer and a struggling actress. The show's form is unique. Cathy starts at the end of the relationship, and tells her story backwards, while Jamie starts at the beginning. The only point of intersection is the middle at their engagement. Early in the relationship, Jamie feels lucky that his book is getting published and is excited about his life with Cathy (**"Moving Too Fast"**). Later he sings **"If I Didn't Believe in You"** while in an argument when Cathy refuses to go to a party being thrown by the publishers of his book.

THE LIGHT IN THE PIAZZA (Broadway 2005)
Music and Lyrics by Adam Guettel

The story, after a novella by Elizabeth Spencer, concerns a wealthy North Carolinian mother, Margaret Johnson and her beautiful, childlike 26-year-old daughter Clara on extended vacation in Florence and Rome in the summer of 1953. Soon after their arrival in Florence, through a chance encounter, Clara meets Fabrizio, a 20-year-old Italian man who speaks little English. Though there is a spark between them, Margaret protectively takes Clara away. Overhearing her mother discussing with her father Clara's upcoming marriage, Clara becomes upset and runs to break it off with Fabrizio. He comforts her in **"Love to Me."** In the end, Clara and Fabrizio will be married.

THE LITTLE MERMAID (Broadway 2008)
Music by Alan Menken
Lyrics by Howard Ashman and Glenn Slater

Based on the Hans Christian Andersen tale, the 1989 animated Disney film *The Little Mermaid* was the basis for the stage musical, with several added songs. Ariel, a young, sea-dwelling mermaid, longs to be human. She falls in love with the human prince and, aided by some magic, gets her wish. **"Her Voice"** was one of the new songs added for the Broadway musical. Eric sings it after he is thrown overboard during a storm in Act I and saved by Ariel, who swims him safely to shore. Eric vows that he will find this woman (actually, a mermaid at that point) who saved his life, though he remembers only her voice and beautiful singing.

LITTLE WOMEN (Broadway 2005)
Music by Jason Howland
Lyrics by Mindi Dickstein

The musical is based on the famous 1869 American novel by Louisa May Alcott about the close-knit March family of Concord, Massachusetts, during and after the Civil War. Four sisters (Jo, Meg, Amy, and Beth) and their mother (Marmee) make the best they can of their lives while the patriarch of the household is serving in the U.S. Army as a chaplain. Laurie, a young man whose grandfather is against him having any relationship with the March family, expresses his hope for friendship with Jo in **"Take a Chance on Me."** He later proposes, and she declines, leaving him heartbroken. Jo lands in New York, where she is an aspiring writer. Laurie winds up marrying Jo's sister Amy. Jo matures as a young woman and a writer, and has a loving relationship with the older Professor Bhaer. The story ends with the announcement that Jo's book, *Little Women*, about her life with her sisters, has found a publisher.

A MAN OF NO IMPORTANCE (Off-Broadway 2002)
Music by Stephen Flaherty
Lyrics by Lynn Ahrens

A Man of No Importance is based on of the 1994 film of the same name, which starred Albert Finney. The musical won the Outer Circle Critics award for Best Off-Broadway Musical. It takes place in Dublin in 1964 and tells of Alfie Byrne, a bus conductor and director of an amateur theatre troupe that has been shut down by Father Kenny, the priest at the church where they rehearse, because he objects to their planned production of Oscar Wilde's *Salome*. Alfie's muse is Wilde, and he quotes him throughout the play. Alfie hides his feelings for the handsome bus driver Robbie Fay, who sings **"The Streets of Dublin"** in Act I. By the end of the show Alfie is able to face himself and who he is as a gay man.

MEMPHIS *(Broadway 2009; London 2014)*
Music by David Bryan
Lyrics by David Bryan and Joe DiPietro

Memphis tells the story of white radio D.J. Huey Calhoun in 1950s segregated Memphis. Huey is harassed for playing black music on white radio stations. His style and the music wins over audiences, however, and he becomes popular. He helps the talented African-American singer Felicia gain a foothold on her career, and also falls in love with her. An interracial relationship such as theirs is unacceptable in Memphis of the era, and leads to Felicia being badly beaten. Huey loses his chance to host a national TV show (à la *American Bandstand*) when he insists on using black dancers. Felicia moves to New York to focus on her career, after explaining to Huey that they could never marry or be together in Memphis. Near the end of the musical, an unemployed and downtrodden Huey sings **"Memphis Lives in Me,"** about his inability to leave his hometown despite the hardships it has caused him.

ONCE *(Off-Broadway 2011; Broadway 2012; London 2013)*
Music and Lyrics by Glen Hansard and Markéta Irglová

Once was adapted from the 2007 film of the same name. Mourning a break up with a girlfriend who has moved to New York, a busker (simply named Guy in the script) sings the heart-wrenching **"Leave"** on the street in Dublin, accompanying himself on guitar. A young Czech woman (simply called Girl in the script) listens to him, moved, and convinces him to continue with music. Over time she encourages him, they form a band together, and he comes back to life. Later she helps Guy get an appointment with a banker, and Guy plays and sings **"Say It to Me Now"** to convince him to loan him money to pursue a music career in New York. The song also expresses Guy's not yet healed heartache.

REPUBLIC
Words and Music by Kait Kerrigan and Brian Lowdermilk

The songwriters' synopsis from *The Kerrigan-Lowdermilk Songbook*: "*Republic* is an adaptation of Shakespeare's *Henry IV* set in Belfast during the 1970s. It follows Sinn Féin political hopeful Henry Patrick O'Byrne and the unlikely political rise of his son, Hal, who is a member of the IRA. Everyone—from Hal's father to his friends and associates—sees Hal as a delinquent who has charm but lacks ambition. In **"Rise,"** we give a nod to Shakespeare's "I know you all..." monologue (*Henry IV, Part I,* I.2) as Hal reveals his lofty ambitions of not only rising above his father's expectations but also bringing peace to his country at any cost." At this writing the show has not had an Off-Broadway production.

SCHOOL OF ROCK *(Broadway 2015)*
Music by Andrew Lloyd Webber
Lyrics by Glenn Slater

The musical is based on the 2003 film. Dewey Finn loses his gig playing guitar in the band *No Vacancy*. Unemployed and with roommates demanding rent, he is desperate. He dreams of becoming a rock star (**"When I Climb to the Top of Mount Rock"**). Principal Rosalie Mullins from Horace Green School calls to offer a substitute teaching position to Dewey's roommate. Dewey, pretending to be the roommate, accepts the job. Dewey develops the students' musical talents in lieu of teaching other subjects, and eventually leads them to perform at the Battle of the Bands.

SOMETHING ROTTEN *(Broadway 2015)*
Music and Lyrics by Wayne Kirkpatrick and Karey Kirkpatrick

Something Rotten is the story of brothers Nick and Nigel Bottom, playrights who are struggling to compete with William Shakespeare, who dominates the theatre scene in London in 1595. The brothers meet a soothsayer who tells them that the real future of theatre involves singing and dancing, and they set out to write a hit musical. In **"Hard to Be the Bard,"** Shakespeare complains about all the attention he receives for being such a star, and all the pressure put on him by the public to keep generating masterpieces.

SPRING AWAKENING *(Off-Broadway 2006; Broadway 2006)*
Music by Duncan Sheik
Lyrics by Steven Sater

This rock musical is based on the 1891 German play by Frank Wedekind, which was banned for decades because of its frankness about teenage sex and suicide. The setting is a provincial German town in the 1890s. Teenagers struggle against strict morals of adults and the lack of instruction and communication about sex and emotion. Melchior is a smart and rebellious young man who is suspicious of the strict school system. His friend Moritz is so distraught when he fails out of school and his father throws him out of the house that he kills himself. At the funeral Melchior blames Moritz's father for his cruelty, and sings **"Left Behind"** about the life that Moritz will never lead.

THOROUGHLY MODERN MILLIE *(Broadway 2002)*
Music by Jeanine Tesori
Lyrics by Dick Scanlan

Based on the 1967 movie starring Julie Andrews, *Thoroughly Modern Millie*, the stage musical retained only three of the songs from the movie (including the title song), with additional score added. It chronicles the life of Millie, a transplanted Kansas girl trying to make it big in New York in the flapper days of 1922. Millie gets a job as a stenographer at the Sincere Trust Insurance Company. She intends to marry her wealthy boss, but falls for a charming but poor paper clip salesman, Jimmy Smith, although Jimmy seems to be interested in her friend, Miss Dorothy. **"What Do I Need with Love"** is Jimmy's song from Act I. After meeting Millie he realizes he has feelings for her, but finds them inconveniently out of step with his plan to play the field. In the end Millie, in love with Jimmy, finds out he is a rich millionaire posing as a pauper.

TUCK EVERLASTING *(Broadway 2016)*
Music by Chris Miller
Lyrics by Nathan Tyson

Previously a book by Natalie Babbitt and two films (1981 and 2002), the musical *Tuck Everlasting* tells the story of 11-year-old Winnie Foster, who runs away from home and discovers a family, the Tucks, living the woods. The Tucks traveled to the area many years earlier and inadvertently drank from a magical spring in the woods that granted them eternal life. Jesse, the youngest of the Tucks, climbs with Winnie through the tall trees that have become familiar to him in **"Top of the World."** Later the Tucks are pursued by a mysterious man in a yellow suit, who wants to bottle and sell the water. The Tuck family leaves Winnie with a small bottle of the water. They must flee but invite her to join them when she is of age and can drink the water. Winnie chooses not to drink and pours it onto a frog. Many years later, the Tucks discover her grave and see the happy life she led.

THE UNAUTHORIZED AUTOBIOGRAPHY OF SAMANTHA BROWN
Music and Lyrics by Kait Kerrigan and Brian Lowdermilk

The songwriters' synopsis from *The Kerrigan-Lowdermilk Songbook*: "Samantha Brown is the valedictorian of her high school and up until this year, she's always had a clear path ahead of her. When her best friend is killed in a car accident. Sam starts to question everything that she knew about herself. Who is she now? When [best friend] Kelly dies, Sam feels like 'real life was the ghost.' Nothing moves her. Nothing wakes her up. Except one thing. She's at the DMV with [boyfriend] Adam, waiting to take her driver's test for the fourth time, when Adam offers a romantic escape from all her problems in **'Run Away With Me.'**" As of this writing the show has not had an Off-Broadway production.

THE WILD PARTY *(Off-Broadway 2000)*
Music and Lyrics by Andrew Lippa

The Off-Broadway musical *The Wild Party* is based on a book-length narrative poem, published in 1928, by Joseph Monocure March. The poem was controversial at the time for its depiction of what was viewed as sexual depravity and was banned in Boston. The story takes place in the 1920s and the two main protagonists are Queenie and her lover Burrs, a promiscuous vaudevillian clown. The two reach a rocky point and decide to throw a party to bring back some excitement to their relationship. The party is attended by a group of artists and homosexuals, and debauchery ensues. Burrs wonders about Queenie's irresistible pull on him in the scintillating vibe of **"What Is It About Her?"** (By coincidence, *The Wild Party* with a score by Michael John LaChiusa opened on Broadway in 2000.)

PROUD OF YOUR BOY

from *Aladdin*

Music by Alan Menken
Lyrics by Howard Ashman

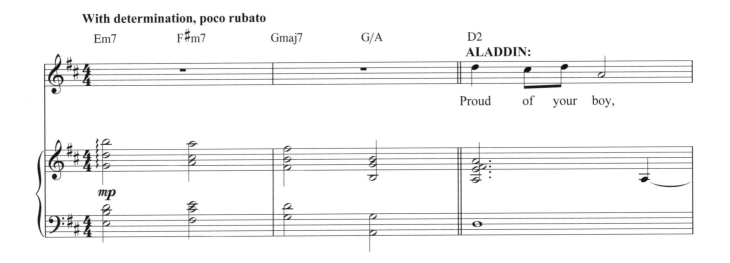

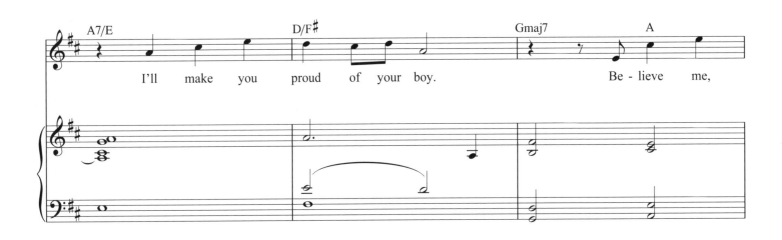

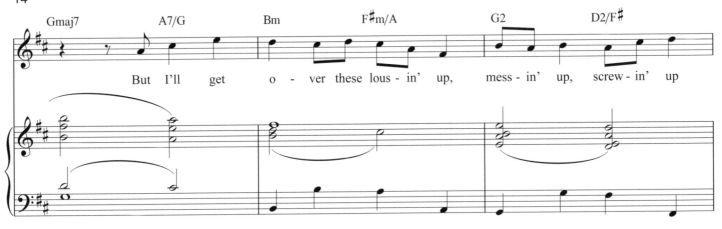

But I'll get o - ver these lous - in' up, mess - in' up, screw - in' up

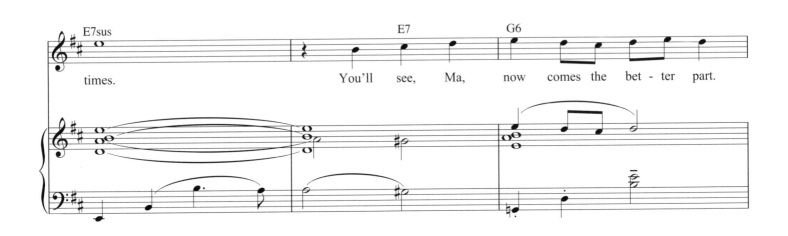

times. You'll see, Ma, now comes the bet - ter part.

Some one's gon - na make good, cross his stu - pid heart... Make good and

Moving forward

fi - nal - ly make you proud of your boy!

Tell me that I've been a louse and a loaf - er, you won't get a fight here, no ma'am. Say I'm a gold - brick, a goof - off, no good, but that could - n't be all that I am. Wa - ter flows un - der the

TRULY ALIVE
from *Amazing Grace*

Music and Lyrics by Christopher Smith

Allegro molto (♩ = 108)

There's a world I___ must see_____

STRANGER
from *Big Fish*

Music and Lyrics by
Andrew Lippa

But still feels_ true. I'm

pass-ing through_ a rite_ that ev - 'ry par-ent does._ I'm

walk-ing on_ some shared_ fa - mil - iar ground._ Yet

ev-'ry step_ I take_ is not a step that was._ And I've

What do I feel?_____ I feel con-nect - ed in a way_ I've nev - er known._ A line from Dad_ to me_ to new-born son. So from to-day_ I'll nev-er make_ a choice a-lone._ One for all, all for one. And

try, I'll real-ly try. And in time my boy is sure to see_ bright-er days_ for Dad and me. We can do_ things bet-ter than be - fore. So that strang - ers we will be_ no more._

IT ALL FADES AWAY
from *The Bridges of Madison County*

Music and Lyrics by
Jason Robert Brown

There was some-thing in a des - ert.___ There was some-place wild and green, And a

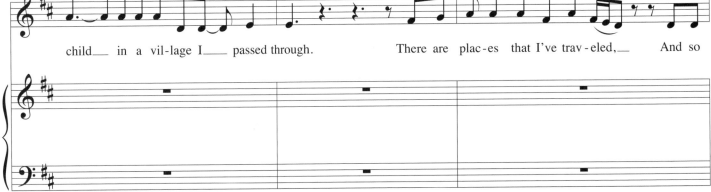

child___ in a vil-lage I___ passed through. There are plac-es that I've trav-eled,___ And so

man - y things___ I've seen, And___ it all fades a - way___ but

ENJOY THE TRIP
from *Bring It On: The Musical*

Music by Tom Kitt
Lyrics by Amanda Green

Driving mid-tempo Pop (♩ = 83)

RANDALL:

I'm a

stud now,___ it's clear so it'-ll shock you___ to hear___ that

I was a to-tal dork___ my fresh-man___ year. I was a

(guitar strum)

HEARTBREAKER

from *Bright Star*

Music by Stephen Martin and Edie Brickell
Lyrics by Edie Brickell

GREAT BIG STUFF

from *Dirty Rotten Scoundrels*

Words and Music by
David Yazbek

Freddy is accompanied by ensemble, eliminated in this solo edition.

56

59

This phrase, sung by ensemble in the show, can be sung one octave higher by Freddy from this point on, each time it occurs.

ev - er! *(Spoken:) I'll change my name, too!* *I'll get my hatchback*

all pimped out. The is - lands in the win - ter, the Hamp - tons in the sum - mer, the

fash - ion plate I date 'll give me hum - mers in my Hum - mer. The cash to keep me id - le, the

chicks to keep me vi - tal, the pills to keep me hap - py e - ven when I'm su - i - ci - dal.

Great big stuff! Nothing crass or crappy. Great big stuff! That would

make me very happy. Great big stuff! Bring it on and make it snappy!

(Spoken:) I want some really classy shit!

Like a mink track suit! *My own personal Zamboni!*

I AM ALDOLPHO
from *The Drowsy Chaperone*

Words and Music by Lisa Lambert
and Greg Morrison

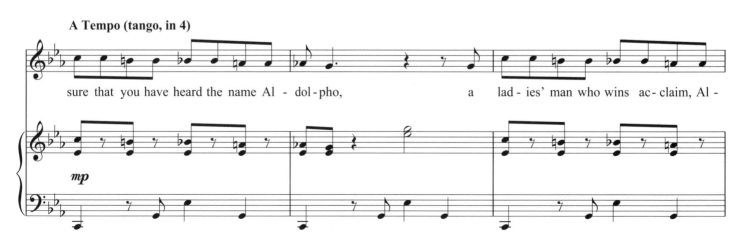

dol-pho. Well, love-ly miss I am the same Al-dol - pho. I in-tro-

duce my-self, I am Al-dol-pho. Not so fast... So

just in case you did-n't hear Al-dol-pho, I'll try to make it ver-y clear: Al-

dol-pho. The love-ly lad-ies al-ways cheer Al-dol - pho when I re-

RIGHT BEFORE MY EYES

from *Ever After*

Music by Zina Goldrich
Lyrics by Marcy Heisler

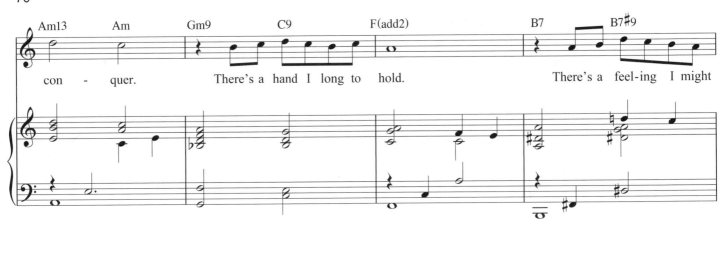

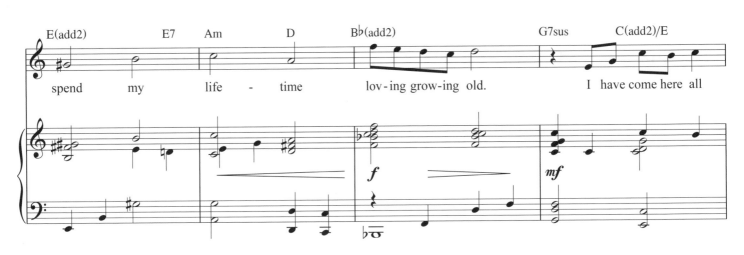

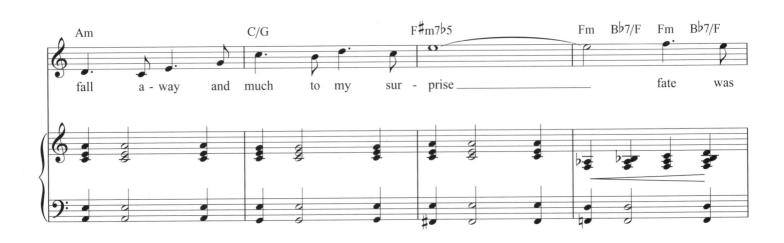

MAN
from *The Full Monty*

Words and Music by
David Yazbek

This version has been adapted as a solo.

8vb throughout

tough. Your smell is scar-y. Here's what you're not you're not a

fair-y. No you're a beer drink-in' real live ___ man.

loco

And when the beef comes out, you do the carv-in'. You

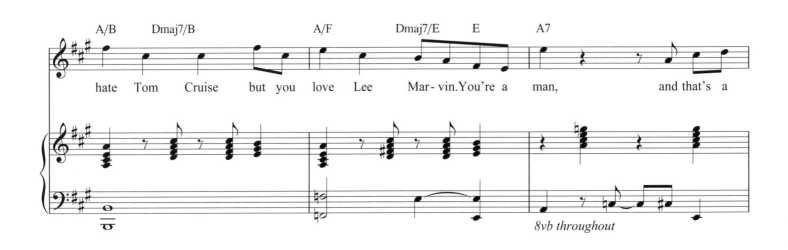

hate Tom Cruise but you love Lee Mar-vin. You're a man, and that's a

8vb throughout

*air guitar this Led Zeppelin lick

SIBELLA
from *A Gentleman's Guide to Love and Murder*

Music by Steven Lutvak
Lyrics by Robert L. Freedman and
Steven Lutvak

Molto rubato

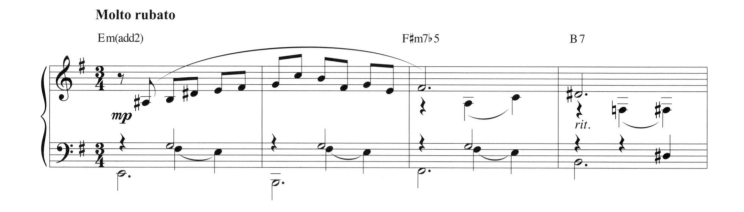

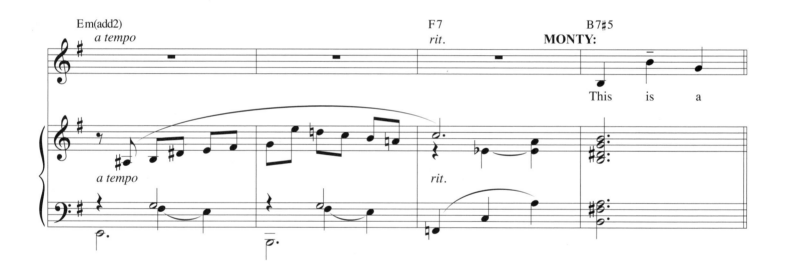

This is a

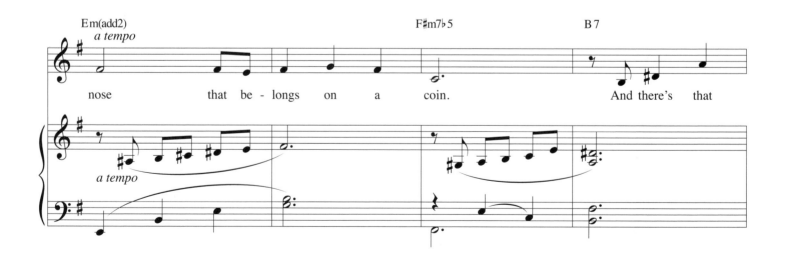

nose that be-longs on a coin. And there's that

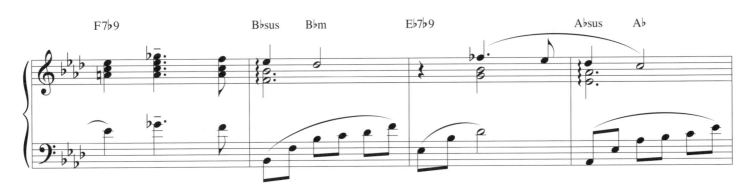

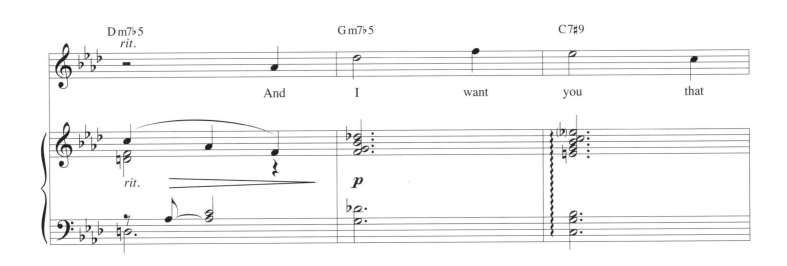

And I want you that

way.

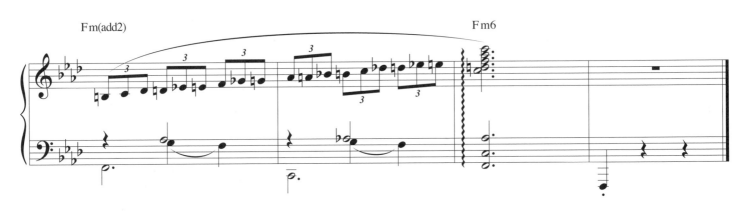

YOU'LL BE BACK

from *Hamilton*

Words and Music by
Lin-Manuel Miranda

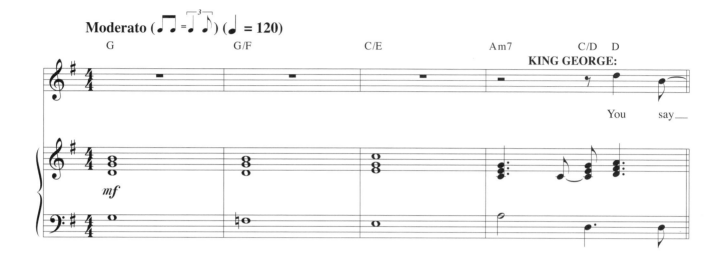

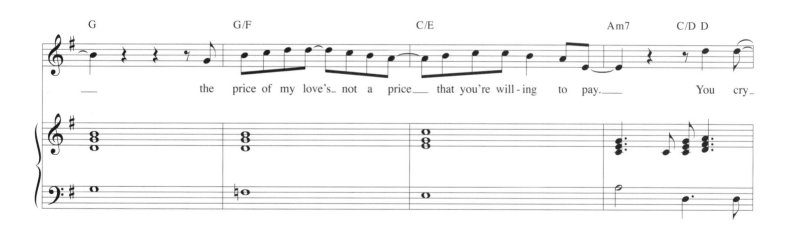

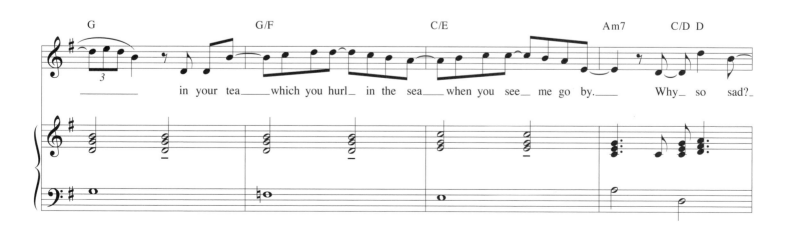

ISN'T THAT ENOUGH?

from *Honeymoon in Vegas*

Music and Lyrics by
Jason Robert Brown

YOU NEVER KNOW

from *If/Then*

Lyrics by Brian Yorkey
Music by Tom Kitt

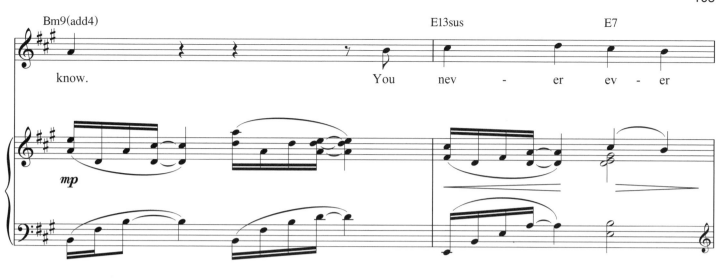

know.   You   nev - er   ev - er

know. _____

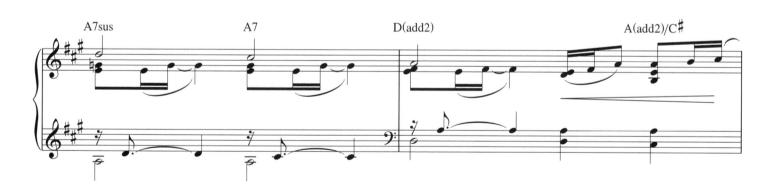

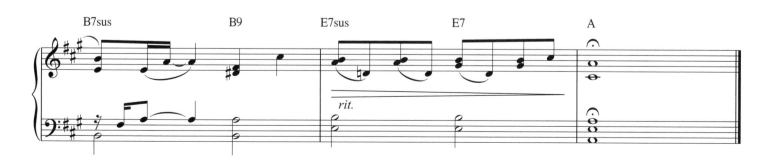

YOU DON'T NEED TO LOVE ME

from *If/Then*

Lyrics by Brian Yorkey
Music by Tom Kitt

Moody yet romantic, expressive (♩ = 131)

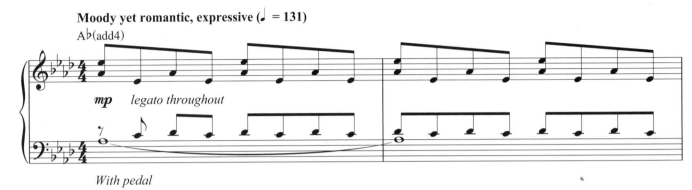

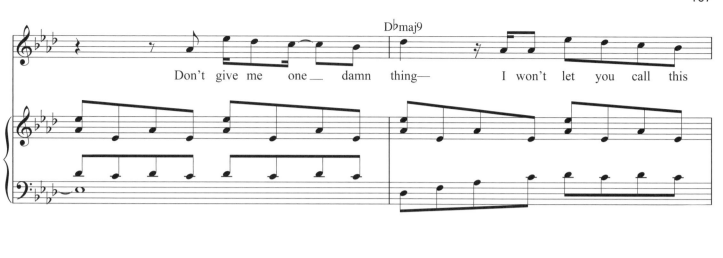

Don't give me one __ damn thing— I won't let you call this

greed— Just let me give to you—__ that's the on-ly thing I need.__

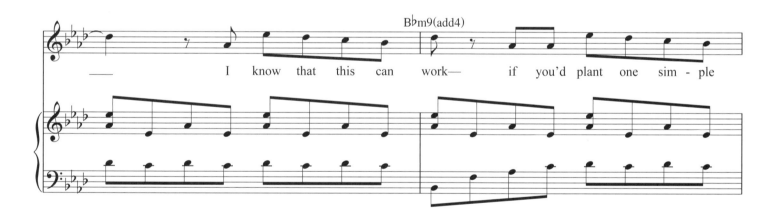

__ I know that this can work— if you'd plant one sim-ple

seed you'd see it grow... You don't need to

We can keep on___ be-ing lone-ly... but we don't have to be

a - part. And I'll nev - er e - ven ask you to

let me have your heart... so I'll nev - er break your

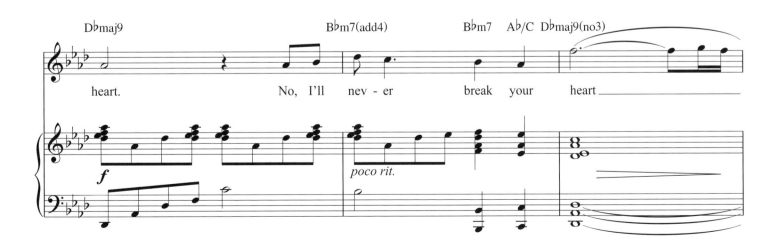

heart. No, I'll nev - er break your heart_____

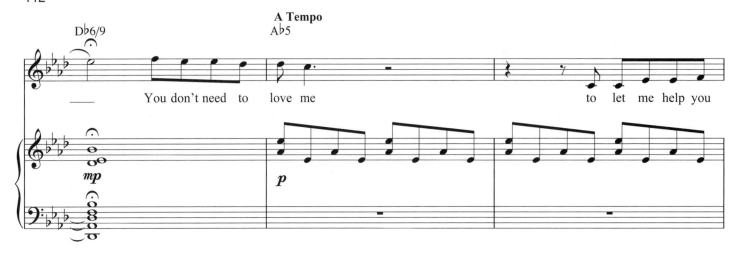

You don't need to love me to let me help you

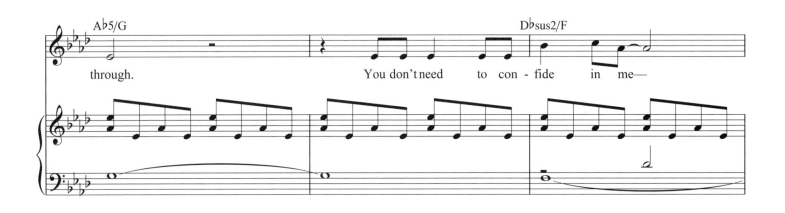

through. You don't need to con-fide in me—

I've got crap e-nough for two. You don't need to

an-swer, I'll know be-fore you do...

But hear me, ___ and be-lieve me, ___

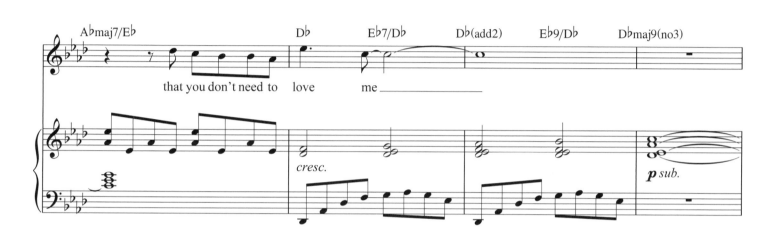

that you don't need to love me ___

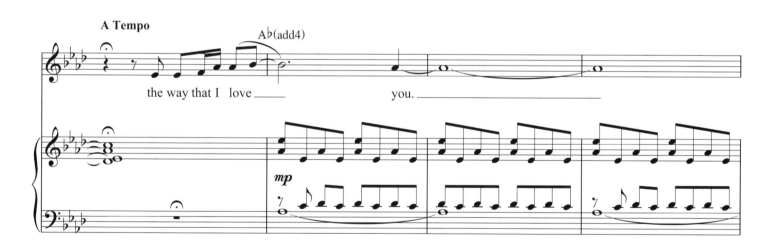

the way that I love ___ you. ___

WHATEVER
from *It Shoulda Been You*

Words by Brian Hargrove
Music by Barbara Anselmi

With tenderness (♩= 76)

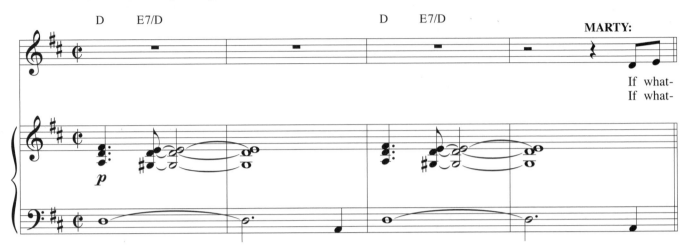

MARTY:

If what-
If what-

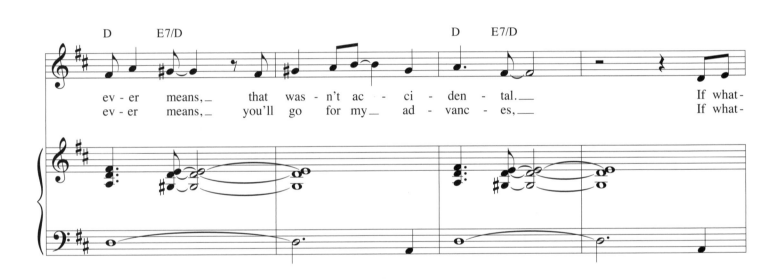

ev - er means,__ that was - n't ac - ci - den - tal.__
ev - er means,__ you'll go for my__ ad - vanc - es,__

If what-
If what-

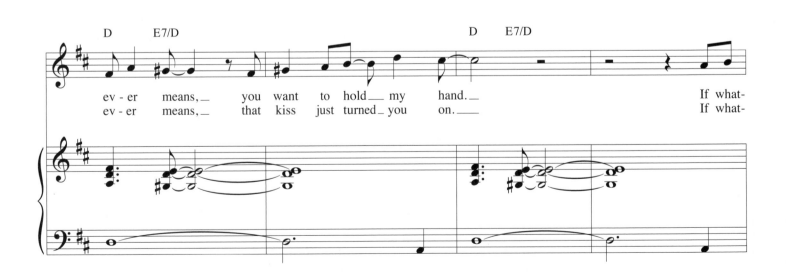

ev - er means,__ you want to hold__ my hand.__
ev - er means,__ that kiss just turned__ you on. __

If what-
If what-

IF I DIDN'T BELIEVE IN YOU

from *The Last Five Years*

Music and Lyrics by
Jason Robert Brown

MOVING TOO FAST
from *The Last Five Years*

Music and Lyrics by
Jason Robert Brown

I'm do - in' things I nev - er dreamed of be - fore!____

(8vb)

Bb7

We start to take the next step to - geth - er,

(8vb)

Found an a - part - ment on Se - ven - ty - Third!___

(8vb)

B7

The *At - lan - tic Month - ly*'s print - ing my first chap - ter–

(8vb)

LOVE TO ME
from *The Light in the Piazza*

Words and Music by
Adam Guettel

Tenderly

no - tice how you hun - ger for sur - prise,

and do not think that you are tall e - nough,

like you're stand - ing on_____ a

moun - tain - side_____ a - lone._____ This is what I

see. _____ Oh _____

_____ Oh _____

_____ You're not _____ a - lone! _____

Now I see as I have nev-er seen _____ be -

fore, _____ since that mo - ment in the

square _____ when your

hat is car - ried in the air _____

just so you can chase it, _____

just so I can be there. This is how I know.

This is what I see. This is love to

me.

rit.

HER VOICE
from Walt Disney's *The Little Mermaid - A Broadway Musical*

Music by Alan Menken
Lyrics by Glenn Slater

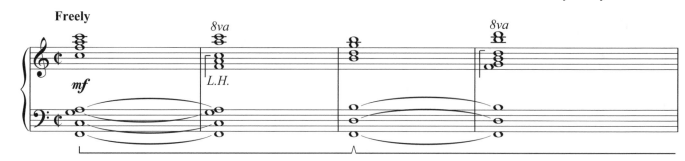

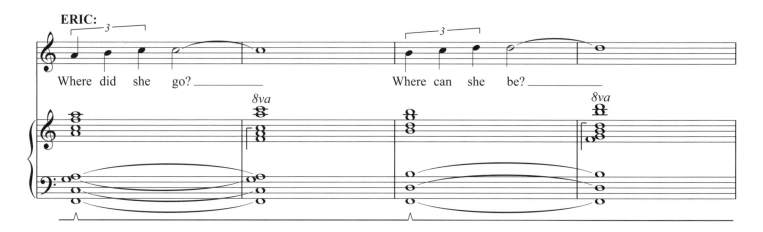

ERIC: Where did she go? Where can she be?

When will she come a-gain, call-ing to me, call-ing to

me, call-ing to me?

Some-where she is sing-ing and her song is meant for me. _____ And her voice, it's sweet as an - gels sigh - ing. _____ And her voice, it's warm as sum - mer sky. _____

rip - ple of the waves a - gainst the shore - line.

I can see her smil - ing in the moon - light as it set - tles on the sand.

I can feel her wait - ing just be - yond the pale ho -

ri - zon, singing out a mel - o - dy too

love - ly to with - stand._____ And her

molto rall.

voice, it's there as dusk is fall - ing._____

a tempo

f a tempo

___ And her voice, it's there as dawn steals

by._____ Pure and bright, it's

parlando

Real as the sea. If you can hear me now, ___ come set me free, ___

rit. *accel.*

___ come set me free! ___

rit. *accel. e cresc.*

a tempo

f a tempo

molto rall.

8va

molto rall. *sfz*

8vb

TAKE A CHANCE ON ME
from the Stage Musical *Little Women*

Music by Jason Howland
Lyrics by Mindi Dickstein

This is ver-y nice, such a love-ly par-ty. The mu-sic sounds so thrill-ing. ___

It makes a per-son feel like danc - ing. ___

(rhythmically steady)

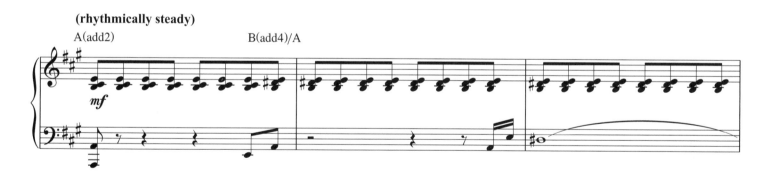

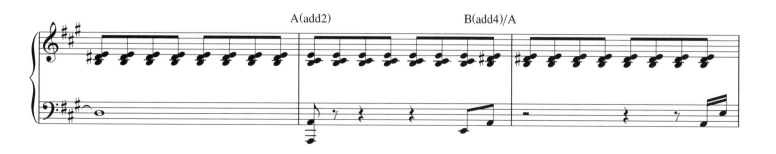

154

THE STREETS OF DUBLIN
from *A Man of No Importance*

Lyrics by Lynn Ahrens
Music by Stephen Flaherty

ROBBIE: There's Tom-my Flan-a-gan who lights the gas lamps... a hun-dred nine-ty lamps in Phoe-nix Park a-lone. He's done it drunk for o-ver fif-ty-sev-en years in Dub-lin!

161

MEMPHIS LIVES IN ME

from *Memphis*

Music by David Bryan
Lyrics by Joe DiPietro and David Bryan

The ensemble parts have been eliminated for this solo version.

SAY IT TO ME NOW
from the Broadway Musical *Once*

Words and Music by Glen Hansard,
Graham Downey, Paul Brennan,
Noreen O'Donnell, Colm Macconiomaire
and David Odlum

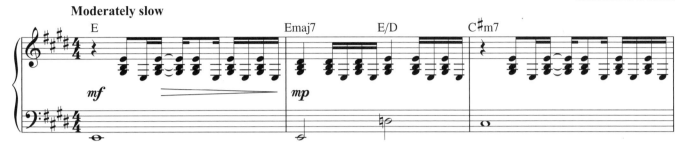

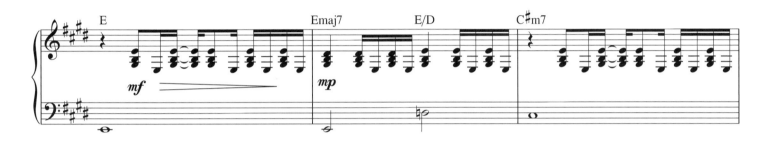

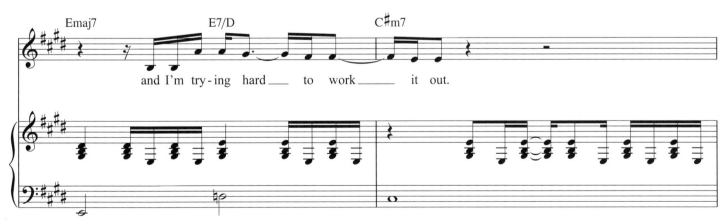

This edition is based on the Broadway original cast recording. The piano part is an idiomatic arrangement for the instrument in the spirit of the cast recording guitar accompaniment.

LEAVE
from the Broadway Musical *Once*

Words and Music by
Glen Hansard

Slowly, in 1 (♩♩ = ♩ ♪ generally)

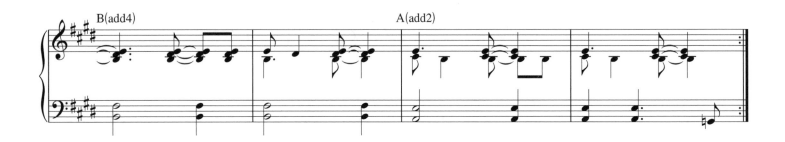

GUY:

"I can't wait for-ev-er,"   is
And I hope you feel bet-ter,

all that you said___   be-fore you stood up.
now that it's out.___   What took you so long?___

This edition is based on the Broadway original cast recording. The piano part is an idiomatic arrangement for the instrument in the spirit of the cast recording guitar accompaniment.

*Pronounced "eye"

RISE
from *Republic*

Words and Music by
Kait Kerrigan
and Brian Lowdermilk

Intense Orchestral Rock (♩ = 150)

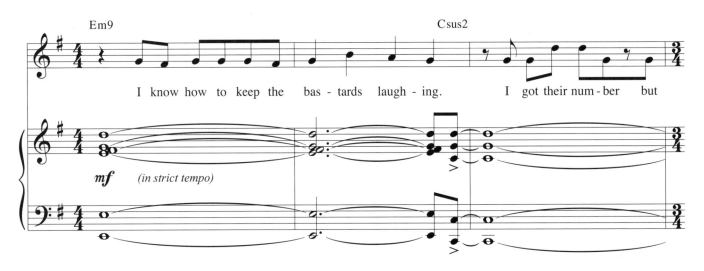

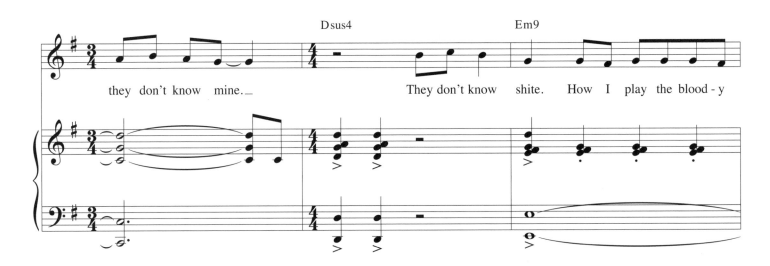

188

HARD TO BE THE BARD

from *Something Rotten*

Words and Music by
Wayne Kirkpatrick
and Karey Kirkpatrick

Rock Shuffle, Swing 8ths (♩ = 111)

Sing Shakepeare's part only for a solo version.

SHAKESPEARE: *Honestly, I don't know how I do it.*
I mean, there's only so much of me that can go around.

SHAKESPEARE: *I know writing made me famous,*
but being famous is just so much more fun.

write down a word, but it's NOT the right word, so you TRY a new word, but you HATE the new word, then you

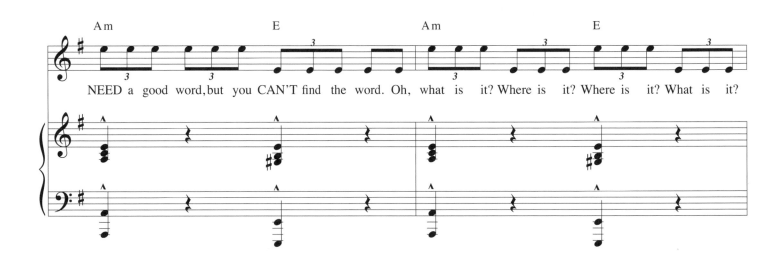

NEED a good word, but you CAN'T find the word. Oh, what is it? Where is it? Where is it? What is it?

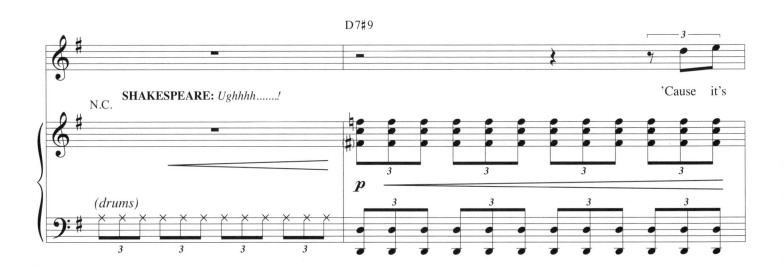

SHAKESPEARE: *Ughhhh.......!*

'Cause it's

A cut has been made for this solo edition.

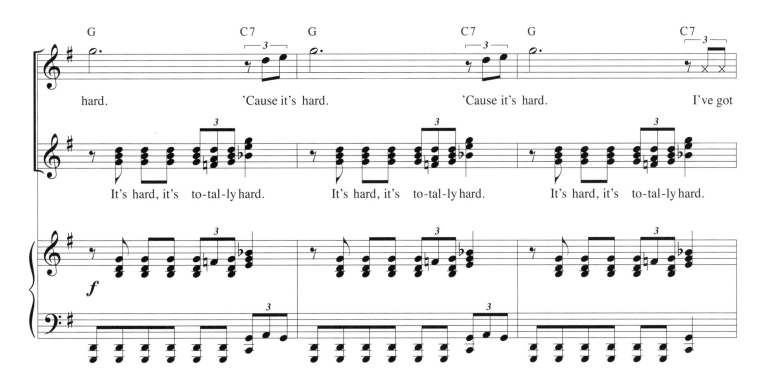

hard.   'Cause it's hard.   'Cause it's hard.   I've got

It's hard, it's to-tal-ly hard.   It's hard, it's to-tal-ly hard.   It's hard, it's to-tal-ly hard.

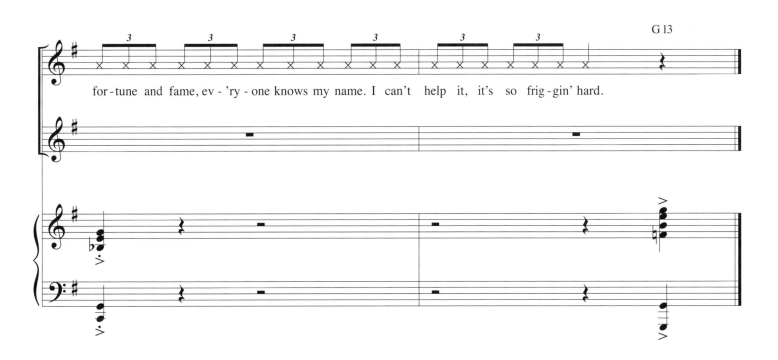

for-tune and fame, ev-'ry-one knows my name. I can't help it, it's so frig-gin' hard.

WHEN I CLIMB TO THE
TOP OF MOUNT ROCK

from *School of Rock*

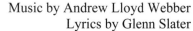

Music by Andrew Lloyd Webber
Lyrics by Glenn Slater

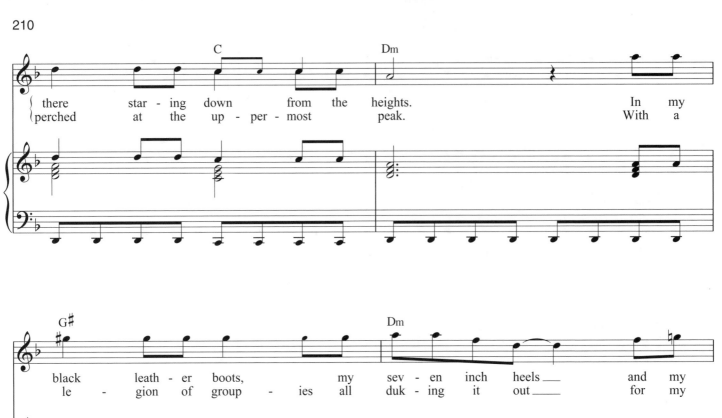

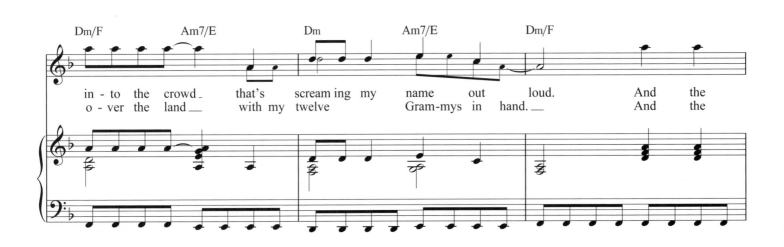

CODA

Slower

'round the top of Mount Rock.

The doub - ters and the hat - ers and the

hip - sters let 'em laugh. Soon they'll all be beg - gin' for my

road - ie's au - to - graph. I know my time is com - in', well,

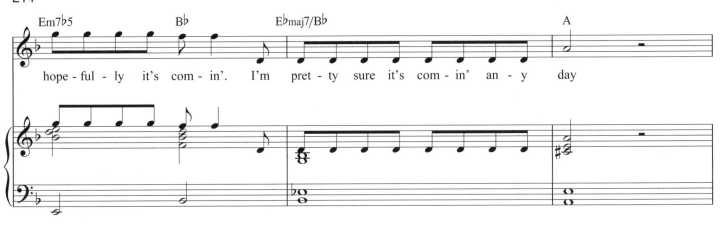

hope - ful - ly it's com - in'. I'm pret - ty sure it's com - in' an - y day

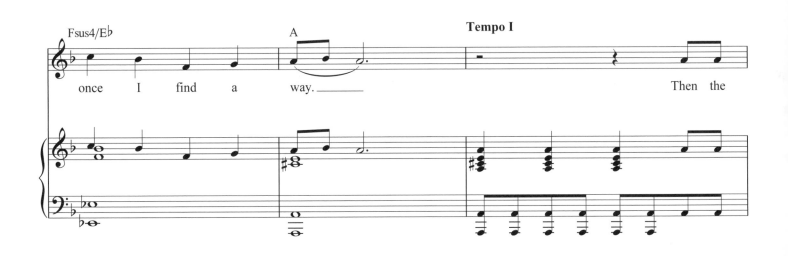

once I find a way. _____ Then the

dreams that I've had ___ since the day I turned ten ___ will be fi - nal - ly com - in' true.

And no one will call ___ me a los - er a - gain ___ or

LEFT BEHIND

from *Spring Awakening*

Music by Duncan Sheik
Lyrics by Steven Sater

Girls match Boys' register, one octave below written

*Girls match Boys' register, one octave below written

shad-ow passed, a shad-ow passed, _ yearn - ing, yearn - ing

for the fool it called a home. _

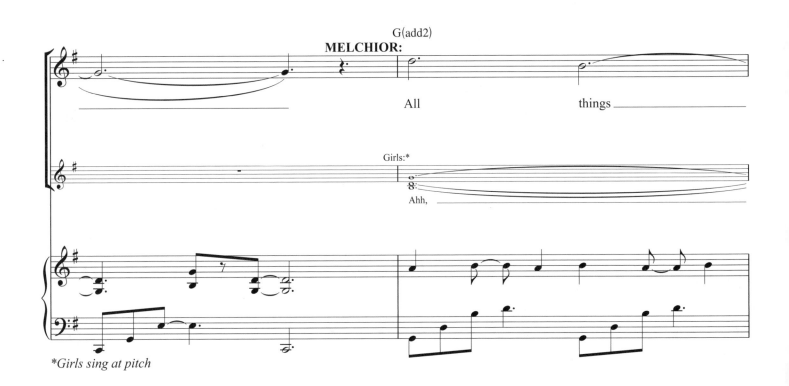

MELCHIOR:

All things _

Girls:*

Ahh, _

*Girls sing at pitch

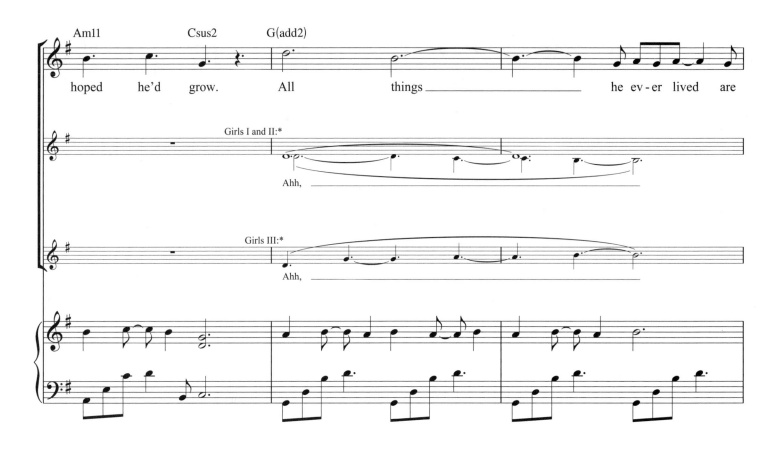

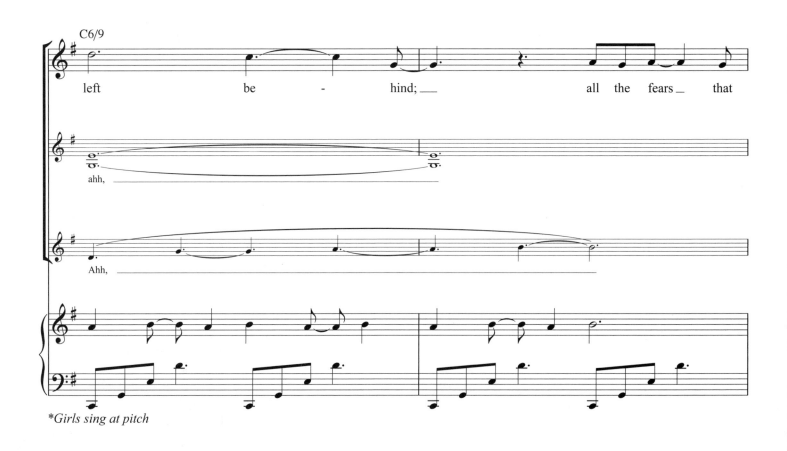

*Girls sing at pitch

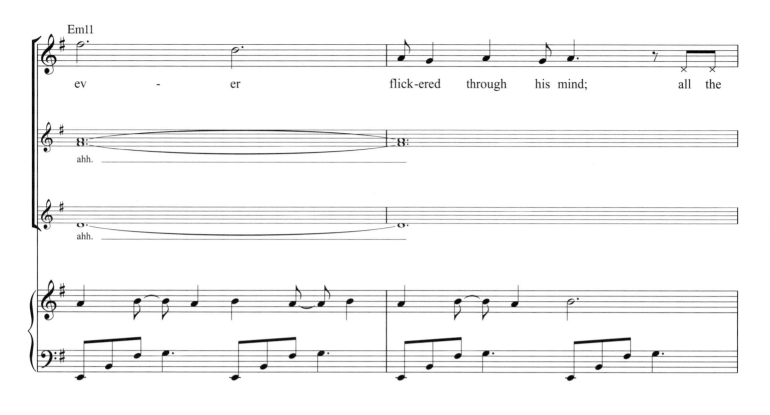

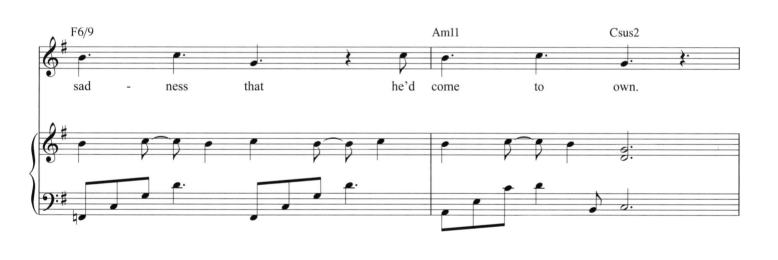

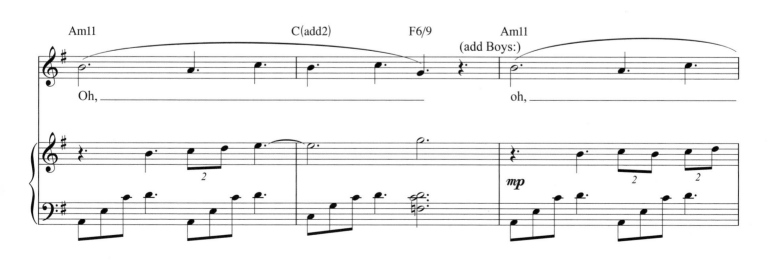

*Girls match Boys' register, one octave below written

*All Girls and Boys sing at pitch

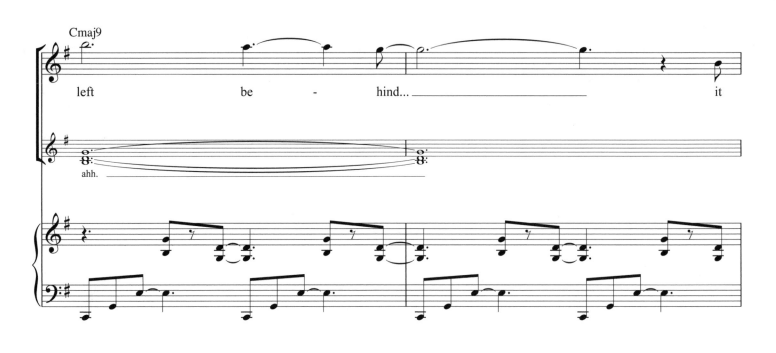

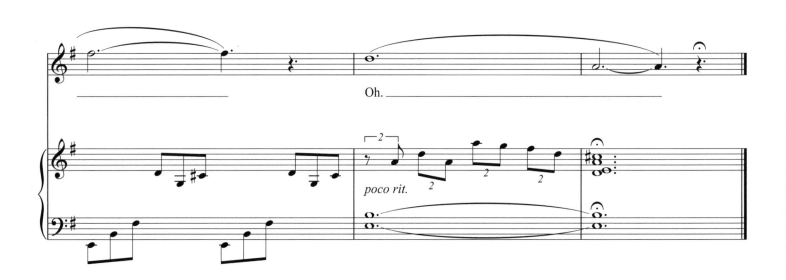

TOP OF THE WORLD
from *Tuck Everlasting*

Music by Chris Miller
Lyrics by Nathan Tysen

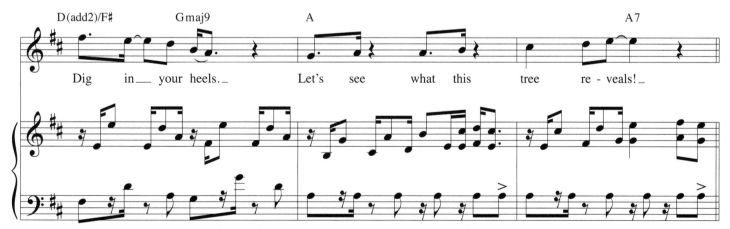

The song begins as a solo, and ensemble is added later. This edition has been adapted as a solo.

230

WHAT DO I NEED WITH LOVE

from *Thoroughly Modern Millie*

Music by Jeanine Tesori
Lyrics by Dick Scanlan

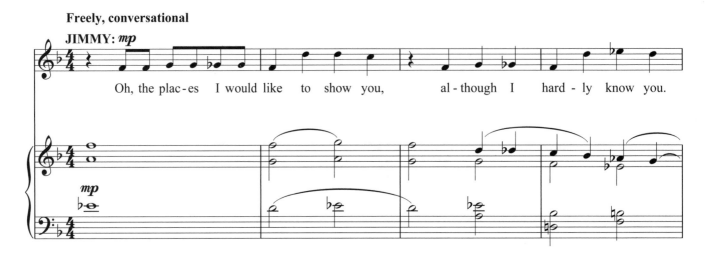

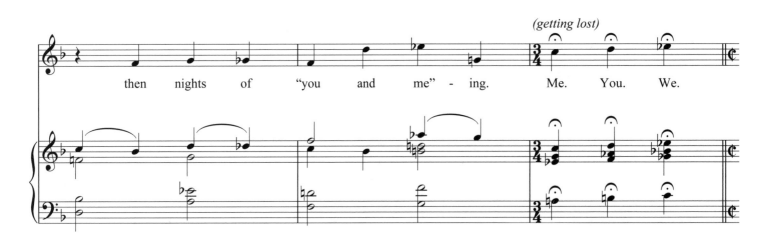

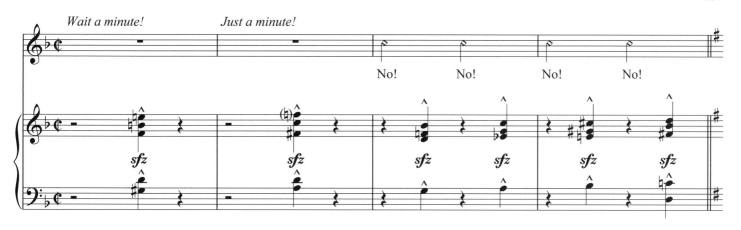

Wait a minute!   *Just a minute!*

No!   No!   No!   No!

A tempo - swingy, in 2

I'm a Joe with just one aim: ___ Ev-'ry night to date a dif-f'rent dame, ___

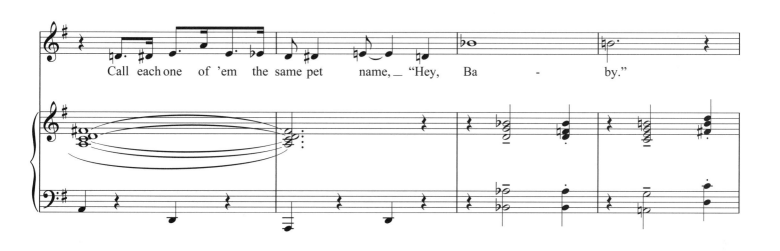

Call each one of 'em the same pet name, ___ "Hey, Ba - by."

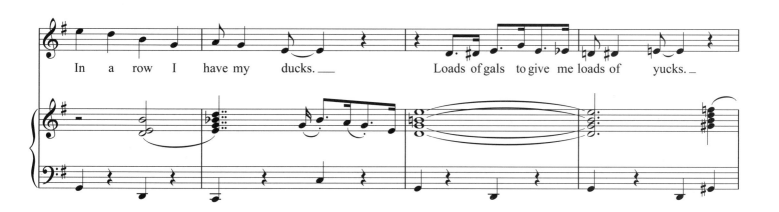

In a row I have my ducks. ___ Loads of gals to give me loads of yucks. ___

Leave the coo - ing to the oth - er clucks. I don't mean may - be.

Got it good. What do I need with love?

Al - ways prac - tice what I preach: keep temp - ta - tion out of eas - y reach.

Stick to dolls who wash their hair in bleach, I'm hap - py.

Come and go the way I choose. _ Nev - er gon - na sing the

tied down blues. _ Oth - er guys _ would kill to fill my shoes. _ No

wing - clipped sap - py! Got it good. _ What do I need _ with

love? _____ That was a near miss.

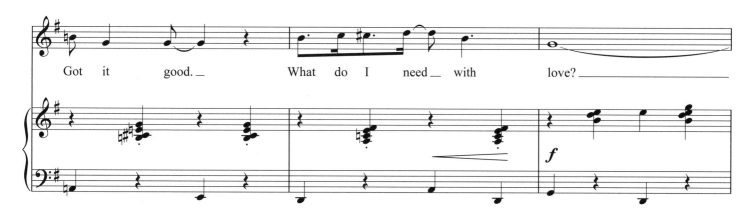

Got it good. ___ What do I need __ with love? _____

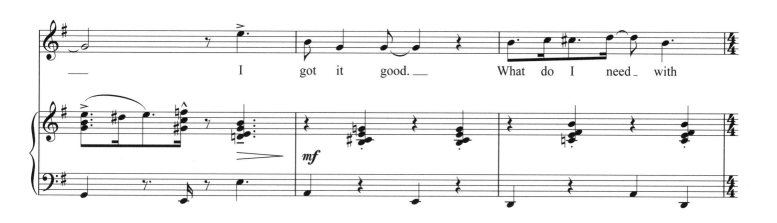

___ I got it good. ___ What do I need _ with

Double time feel - Straight 8ths

"Jolson"

love? _____ Skip the vows and

all that rot. ___ Tell the min - is - ter that "I ___ do" __ not.

RUN AWAY WITH ME

from *The Unauthorized Autobiography of Samantha Brown*

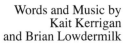

Words and Music by
Kait Kerrigan
and Brian Lowdermilk

Steady, in 1 (♩.= 60)

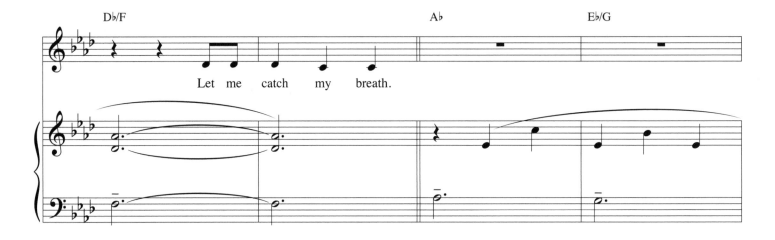

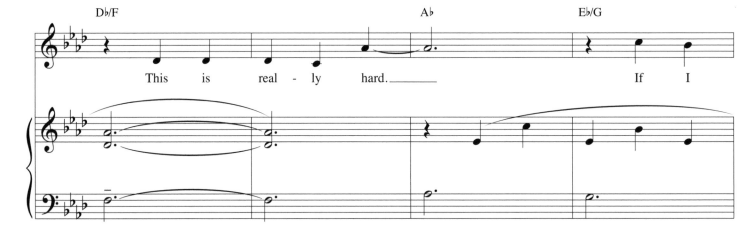

Let me catch my breath.

This is real - ly hard._____ If I

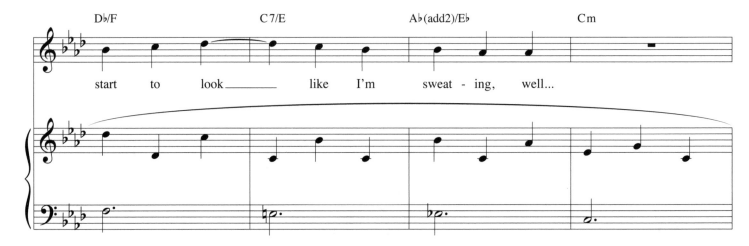

start to look_____ like I'm sweat - ing, well...

WHAT IS IT ABOUT HER?
from *The Wild Party*

Words and Music by
Andrew Lippa

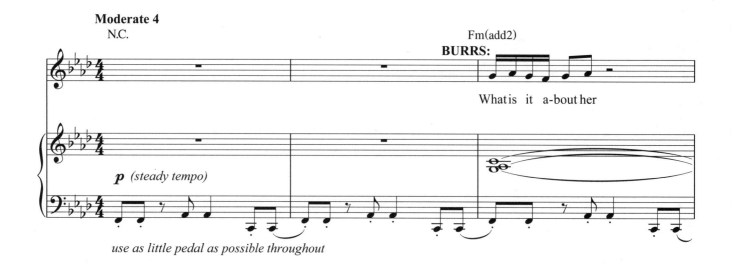

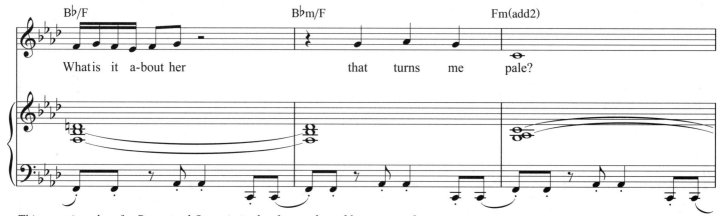

This song is a duet for Burrs and Queenie in the show, adapted here as a solo.

What is it a-bout her that tips the

scale? This girl is all I have

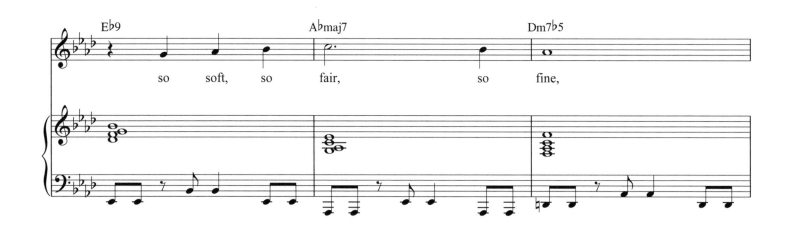

so soft, so fair, so fine,

and she's for - ev - er___ mine.

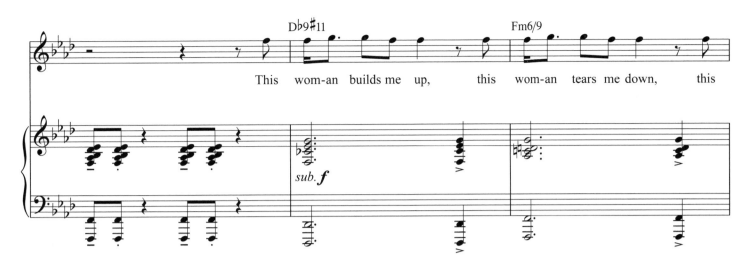

This wom-an builds me up, this wom-an tears me down, this

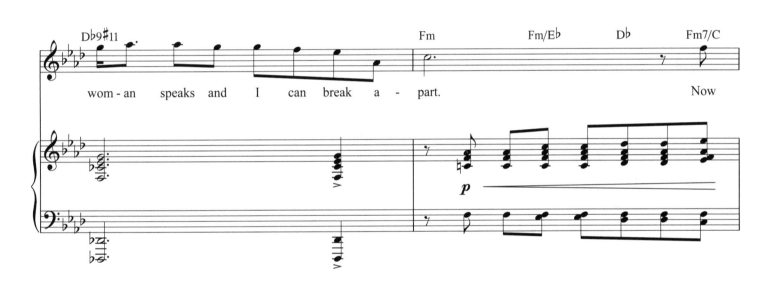

wom-an speaks and I can break a - part. Now

comes an-oth-er man pre-tend-ing he can win her heart, well,

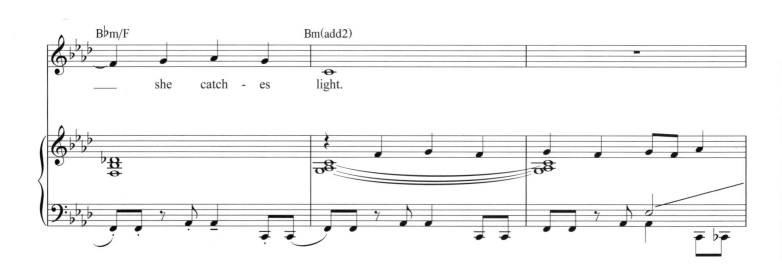

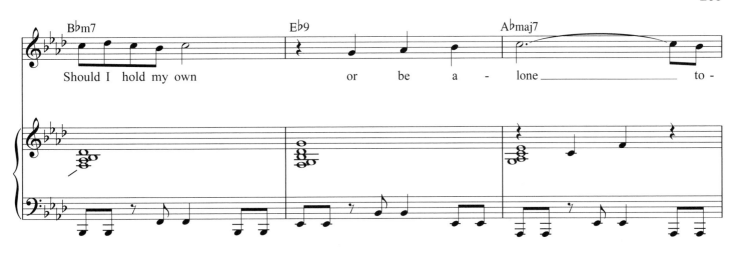

Should I hold my own or be a - lone _____ to -

night? What is it a-bout her that jum-bles feel-ings in - side?

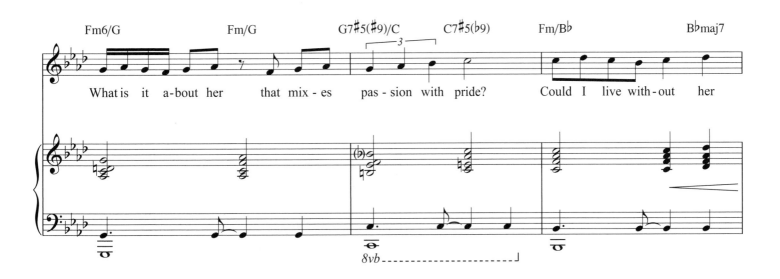

What is it a-bout her that mix-es pas - sion with pride? Could I live with-out her

and let her go? _____ How

Colla voce

loud must I scream NO! _____

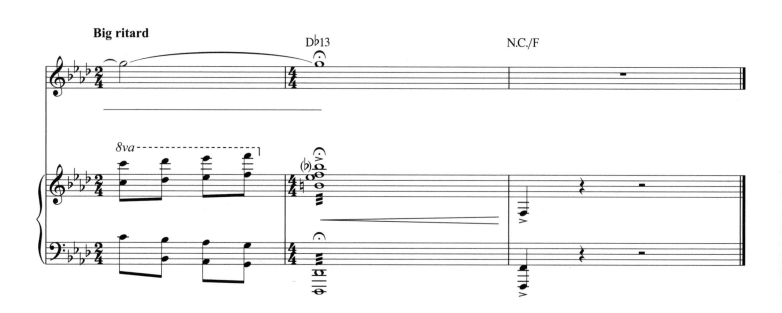

Big ritard